LOOKING FOR HENRY

# LOOKING *for* HENRY

CLIVE DOUCET

EDITED BY
RAMSAY DERRY

THISTLEDOWN PRESS

Canadian Cataloguing in Publication Data

Doucet, Clive, 1946–
Looking for Henry
A poem.
ISBN 1-895449-91-X
1. Letendre, Henry — Poetry. I. Title
PS8557.O787 L66 1999    C811'.54    C99-920119-0
PR9199.3.D566 L66 1999

Cover painting *Plains Cree* by Henry Letendre.
Historical chart image courtesy of Compusult Limited,
Mount Pearl, Newfoundland.
Typeset by Thistledown Press Ltd.
Printed and bound in Canada

NOTE: *The publisher and author have tried, without success, to locate Henry Letendre, whose painting appears on the cover. The publisher would appreciate any information about Henry Letendre's recent or present whereabouts.*

Thistledown Press Ltd.
633 Main Street
Saskatoon, Saskatchewan
S7H 0J8

 Canadian    Patrimoine
Heritage    canadien

Thistledown Press gratefully acknowledges the financial assistance of the Canada Council for the Arts, the Saskatchewan Arts Board, and the Government of Canada through the Book Publishing Industry Development Program for its publishing program.

## ACKNOWLEDGEMENTS

The song quoted in "Chanson Acadienne" on page 85 was written in the 1930s by Loubie Chiasson and appears in *Chéticamp histoire et traditions acadiennes* by Father Anselme Chiasson, Éditions des Aboiteaux, Moncton, 1961.

Some pieces from *Part I: My Beloved People* were previously broadcast on the CBC radio program *Morningside.*

# CONTENTS

# INTRODUCTION

After I wrote *Looking for Henry*, my first readers asked all kinds of questions that I did not expect. What does the word métis mean? Why do you spell it Métis and métis? Where is Acadie? Is there a difference between an Acadien and a Québecois? And it struck me that it is not only the spoils that go to the victors, but also the history. In Canada there were two victors, the French Canadian élite of Québec and the English Canadian elites of the Maritimes and Upper Canada. It is this history of the victors which Canadian children learn. The history of the vanquished or marginalized peoples, the Acadien, the Métis, the Cree and Mi'kmaq, remain as obscure footnotes to the dominant story. Their historic realities are difficult to comprehend today because it is not just the past, but other possibilities for the present that have been extinguished by their subjugation. The present defines the past, as much as the past defines the present. History and myth blend into a self-fulfilling tautology in which the present exists as the only reality possible.

The histories of the Métis and the Acadiens are complex. Laying them out here would risk drowning the poems in a cascade of dates and historical events. All I can hope to do is explain a little about how the poems came about and sketch the background as I see it.

A few years ago, I was invited by Thistledown Press to read from my work at some schools in Saskatoon. I have been writing since I was in my twenties but I am not well known, and to be invited to read with other poets in a place far from my own home was a great compliment. I had never been to Saskatchewan before and I had an easterner's postcard image in my head of flatness of landscape and character. From the beginning, I was surprised. The city of Saskatoon hugs a sharp, dramatic river valley. The countryside rolls to the north and the sky is extraordinary. It is like a sea sky, a vast and luminous vault of the heavens. The city itself has the comfortable feel of civility and civilization with the presence and long history of the aboriginal people to give it a richness of place and character that many eastern cities do not have.

The trip itself turned into one of those rare, defining experiences that re-orient one's view of the world. The Saskatchewan poet, Glen Sorestad, took us out to visit Batoche, the site of the last battle in 1885 between the Métis people and the Canadian government forces under General Middleton. I knew very little about the Métis except that Louis Riel, their political leader, had been hung after the battle for treason, and that Gabriel Dumont, their military leader, had escaped to the United States.

Batoche is about an hour's drive from Saskatoon. It is situated on a small plateau above a cliff overlooking the South Saskatchewan River. There you can still see signs of the old Métis fields in the narrow fence lines that go up from the river and across the plateau. To my surprise, it was a landscape that felt like home, like my father's and grandfather's Acadien village in Cape Breton where I had spent some of my childhood. There was the same long, narrow shape to the fields, the same white clapboard church, the same sense of a plateau and small farms isolated from the modern world. As we began to walk across the battlefield the feelings that swept over me became so intense that I became mute, as if I were listening to ghosts.

The ground was different, the earth much softer, and richer than it was back home. I took my shoes off and ran over the ground barefoot like a child, amazed at the velvet feeling of the deep, prairie soil and at the intense and complex awareness of being at a pivotal place in the evolution of our nation.

It was the strangest thing. I knew very little of the Métis story but I was overcome with this tremendous sense of a shared experience. The power of that visit to Batoche came as much from the unexpectedness of these feelings as from the place itself. I had never really thought about it before, but the first métis marriages in Canada between Aboriginal people and Europeans were probably Acadiens. My line of the Doucet family is descended from some Mi'kmaq grandmothers. The Acadiens, like the western Métis, were caught in the crunch of expanding empires, defeated by the same constellation of European commercial, cultural and military forces that left no room for non-conforming societies. Both were eventually displaced from their farms and villages where they had enjoyed freedom of movement, ownership of their land, and independence of political opinion and of community, to become refugees — to survive later as marginalized people in areas at the extreme edges of their old territories.

These connections and familiar resonances surrounded me throughout my visit. The founder of Batoche was a man called Leandre Letendre (dit Batoche) and on the wall at Thistledown Press were powerful, brooding portraits of early aboriginal leaders by a Métis artist named Henry Letendre. As I looked up at them, I found myself wondering if Henry Letendre was related to Leandre Letendre in the same way that the Doucets are related to Paul-Marie Doucet who was the first Doucet after the exile to settle at Chéticamp on Cape Breton Island. I didn't know if I would ever get the chance to visit Saskatchewan again and it suddenly seemed important to find this artist named Henry Letendre. I wanted to meet him so we could compare our stories and how we felt about our backgrounds.


I have come to realise that Acadien and Métis societies were different from New France and New England which were dominated by various corporate forces. The Europeans who were the ancestors of the Acadien and Métis people did not arrive in Nova Scotia or the Canadian West in a sudden, overwhelming wave of immigration which displaced the original peoples, but in quite small numbers, and the communities they established grew mainly by the natural increase of their own families. As a result both societies evolved in a slow, comparatively harmonious way with the original inhabitants.

In the west, the English and the French Métis combined the hunting and trapping life of the First Nations with European-style farming and village life. The Indian Way and the church steeple were not incompatible for them. Nor were the different languages. The Métis were bilingual and often multilingual. Gabriel Dumont spoke six languages. Riel spoke French, Cree, Assiniboine, and English. The faces in the 1870 photograph of Louis Riel's provisional government tell the story clearly enough. There are men like Louis Riel who look European and men with dark faces who would have looked utterly at home in Sitting Bull's war council. They were neither: they regarded themselves as Métis, not French or English or Indian, but a new nation of the plains.

When, in 1869, Canada acquired the vast western territory of Rupert's Land which had been controlled by the Hudson's Bay Company, the intention was to govern the new territory like a colony until there was a large enough population of immigrants to justify local government. There were by this time about 25,000 Indians in the west and 15,000 English and French-speaking Métis. The French-speaking Métis in particular, who were concentrated around Red River and were led by Louis Riel, resented this arbitrary arrangement. Instead of being treated as subjects, they wanted to bargain independently with the government in Ottawa to define their place in the new nation. They temporarily seized Fort Garry and during this time captured, tried and executed Thomas Scott, an Orangeman who was part of the pro-Canada faction in the region. As a result of Riel's resistance, the province of Manitoba was established and some of his demands were met. But there was a huge influx of new settlers, many of whom treated the Métis as a defeated people and effectively drove them out of the region. Fifteen years later the Métis, now re-established in Saskatchewan and again led by Riel, attempted to resist having their territory overrun yet again, and repeated their demands for local self-government and representation in Ottawa. In 1885, the resistance led to war and defeat.

After the final battle at Batoche followed by Riel's trial and execution, Prime Minister John A. Macdonald made the federal government's policy of cultural extinction very clear: "If they are Indian, they go with the tribe; if they are half-breeds, they are white." As long as Riel had been alive, Macdonald had not had the nerve to utter this policy publicly.

I share the conviction that in the Métis defeat and dispersal, Canada missed the opportunity to be a different kind of nation: one of the few places on the planet where people of aboriginal descent would have been central to the formation of the new government, not crushed by it. This was a tragedy not just for the Métis but for Canada because only very rarely does there occur that happy coincidence of individual character, ideas and opportunity that can move humanity suddenly and boldly forward into a new and better space.

Louis Riel and the Métis, with their provisional government, their Bill of Rights, their readiness to be citizens of Canada but on terms that they negotiated, not terms imposed upon them, were a people and an idea of that new civil order. If they had been matched by an equal vision from the east, instead of the institutionalized bigotry typified by the Loyal Orange Lodge, if they had been matched by federal politicians courageous enough to have fought for what was just and not what was expedient, the stage would have been set for a very different Canada: one where the Métis and aboriginal peoples of the west would have been recognised for what they were, a founding nation of the new nation emerging around them. This was never allowed to happen and it was a great and terrible sadness that it did not. No amount of modern legal wrangling over the Métis provisional government's trial and execution of Thomas Scott will ever change this.

Until I visited Batoche, I had only the vaguest understanding of these issues and it had not occurred to me to connect them to the Acadien experience of my forebears. A hundred and fifty years earlier than the Métis, the Acadiens had also evolved into a distinct, new society in North America with independent views of themselves and their place in the world.

The Acadien community dates first from 1604 when a small number of French settlers established themselves in present-day Nova Scotia at Port Royal on what is now called the Bay of Fundy. They got along with the local Mi'kmaqs and there was some intermarriage. They were at the edge of French-controlled territory and vulnerable to the swaying struggle between France and England for supremacy in North America. For a time, between 1654 and 1670, the English controlled the area and the Acadiens had no contact at all with France. At this time there were less than a thousand of them. After 1670, a few more French families settled in the region and in the next generations the population increased greatly and settlements were established around the Bay of Fundy. The Acadiens flourished until 1755 when the world as they knew it came to an end.

Later, in the nineteenth century, the tragedy of Acadie would be recreated in literature by the New England poet Henry Wadsworth Longfellow with his famous Evangeline. The saintly Evangeline and Acadie have become synonymous, as if old Acadie was entirely populated by mooning, star-crossed lovers wearing quaint, Norman peasant costumes. But prior to the expulsion in 1755, the image in France of Acadie and the Acadiens was very different. In Paris newspapers, cartoons lampooned a half-naked "Acadien" dressed entirely in Indian attire, carrying a bow and arrow. These former Frenchmen had "gone native". It wasn't intended as a compliment. In a letter of November, 1714, the French Governor of the great fortress of Louisbourg on Isle Royale, as Cape Breton was known, complained to his minister at Versailles that the Acadiens were "selfish, idle people, having adopted the habits of the Indians". He advised his minister against buying their aid, stating, "it would be better to purchase slaves."

This stereotype was as far from the truth as was Longfellow's portrait of Acadie as a bucolic heaven. The reality was, the Acadiens were egalitarian and democratic at a time when neither were considered virtues. They followed a complicated seasonal round of activities which included fishing, hunting and trading with the Mi'kmaq people, business with the Bostonnais (as they knew the New Englanders) as well as the care of a sophisticated farming system. They had built a large network of dikes which circled the Bay of Fundy and had successfully harnessed for agriculture one of the largest salt marshes on the planet. All of this had resulted in a quality of individual and family life superior to anything farmers in Europe had been able to achieve. The reality was the Acadiens were prosperous and didn't need or want to work for anyone but themselves. They were independent of both the English and French colonial powers.

And, as it is clear from the angry note of the Governor of Isle Royale to his minister, the Acadiens had little patience for the machinations of Versailles. They called the aristocratic Governors and Intendants who governed Isle Royale and Quebec the "ancien régime", fifty years before the French revolution made this expression fashionable in France.

The French governor at Louisbourg was concerned about the Acadiens because in 1714, France and Great Britain in the Treaty of Utrecht attempted to demarcate their holdings in North America at the end of the first wave of military struggle. The English regained control of mainland Nova Scotia, and thus most of the area inhabited by the Acadiens, while France held on to Isle Royale. French officials tried to persuade the Acadiens to move up to Isle Royale but, having established themselves very successfully in the soft, fertile land around the Bay of Fundy, they declined.

So the Acadiens, by language and origin French, again found themselves living in an English-controlled territory. They formally declared themselves neutral in their village assemblies. For the next thirty years they managed to maintain this position with considerable success, balancing off the French at Louisbourg, the English in Halifax, the Mi'kmaq's in the country around them and their aggressive trading partners the Bostonnais.

But for all their independence of spirit and community, they were extremely vulnerable because they were without allies. Like the Métis, whose farms and communities could be "sold along with the buffalo" when the Hudson's Bay Company turned over its western land to the new Canadian government, the Acadiens had no clerical hierarchy, no corporate business community, no military regiments to negotiate on their behalf with the great powers. And just as John A. Macdonald was not prepared to accept the Métis as an independent people, neither was the British Governor Lawrence in Halifax ready to accept the Acadiens as anything more than a problem to be dealt with.

The renewed threat of war between France and Britain gave Governor Lawrence in Halifax the means, with the militia from Boston, and the perfect excuse, to get rid of these irritating neutral French. In the summer of 1755, without consulting the British government, he ordered their expulsion. Every Acadien community was to be emptied. By this time there were nearly 13,000

Acadiens. By the end of the year about half of them had been rounded up and deported. Apart from the few who escaped, the rest were sent off in the next few years, for the process of deportation continued until 1763. They were scattered without plan to the British colonies along the Atlantic seaboard, to the West Indies and South America as well as to Louisiana. Some went to France, but they found it oppressive and moved on to Louisiana which became the main gathering place for the exiled Acadiens.

The bitter term "ethnic cleansing" had yet to be coined but that is what it was when all the Acadien men, women and children were expelled from their homelands. The object of the deportations, which separated families and flung people as far away as the Falkland Islands, was not physical genocide but, as with the Métis, it was a cultural assault, intended to disperse the Acadien communities into such small fragments that they could never again reassemble into an independent economic or cultural force.

Meanwhile, the Battle of the Plains of Abraham at Québec City in 1759 signalled the final defeat of France in North America. In the aftermath, the French religious, business and military leaders in Québec negotiated a deal with the British which was convenient to both elites. The Québecois were forced to live under a British regime, but were not expelled like the Acadiens, and were able to keep their language, property, religion, education system and business affiliations.

There was no "deal" for the Acadiens. Their former rich farmlands were resettled, and there was no place for them in the new order. But over the next decades, many of them did return, surreptitiously re-establishing their communities in the more remote regions of Nova Scotia and New Brunswick. And it is from those people that the present day Acadiens are descended.

*Looking for Henry*, in a way, is my answer to Longfellow's *Evangeline*. It is written from the perspective of the Acadien exile which began with the deportation in 1755 and which continues to resonate in the lives of Acadiens today, as does, for the Métis, the defeat and dispersal after Batoche.

A poem should speak for itself. The guide must be your own eyes and feelings, but perhaps it would not be intrusive to explain the form of the poems. It follows the Plains Indian tradition of looking for common ancestors and common memories when one family came unexpectedly upon another during the nomadic season. When this occurred, the two groups would camp together and for several days they would talk about relatives, friends and places, attempting to establish points of contact. Once these friendships or points of contact had been established, the families might hunt or travel together for a while if the abundance of game permitted. If no common memories could be established there would be a rupture and perhaps fighting.

Some poem titles are repeated. This is for a reason. The European notion of progress is that things are always moving forward, that there are always new goals to be accomplished, that there are always new titles. In the aboriginal world there is not the same assumption that life is linear, bounded by the process of forming straight lines, marked with beginnings, middles and ends: that we are, as Descartes said, what we think, or as the existentialists claim, what we choose. Instead, it has something to do with an ability to stare quietly into the eye of the universe, to be both where you are and elsewhere.

I never did find Henry Letendre. *Looking for Henry* is my side of the conversation between us that we might have had.

PART I
MY BELOVED PEOPLE

## WAITING

I was wondering
when you would come back.
I was wondering when
you would come paddling
over the water,
the canoe balanced
like a dry leaf
on the clear membrane
of the lake.

It is a strange thing
to sit here
waiting for you,
waiting for someone
I have never met,
waiting for our memories
to align themselves
in some perfect order.

I keep thinking of the fields.
The fields
which your ancestors
laid down in Batoche
and mine in Cape Breton.
The same shape,
long, narrow strips of green
running up
from the river,
running up from the sea.
Even after all these years,
the outline is still there,
the imprint of fence line
on the land.

How did we get to have
the same fields,
with little white churches
framed against the sky?

GRAND ÉTANG

## Grand Étang

There is a photograph
in my father's house.
The village of Grand Étang
from baby to great-grandparent
lined up
in front of the
church.
It is a long, rectangle
of a photograph
spanning the dining room wall.
A mountain of Sunday dinners
have passed beneath
that photograph.

The people of Grand Étang
arranged in proper order.
They stand in neat rows
in front of the church,
ecclesiastical children
for the visit of the Bishop.
He sits at the centre,
a plump, bulldog man,
earnest, young priests on either side,
then altar boys in white gowns
like bright struts on the ribs of a fan.
The people in humble lines behind,
their faces blurred
in sepia tones.

My father's finger
passes slowly along
the rows of faces
burned deep brown by the sun
from a life spent out of doors,

their hands rough and broad.
He pauses here and there
at people he remembers:

> There is Magloire.
> Your great-great-grandfather.
> He used to live in a big house
> on the cliff above the harbour.
> I remember him, says father,
> but not my grandfather.
> He died
> when we were only young.

He stops at the image
of some small children
and turns to me:

> You are
> Clive à Fernand,
> à William à Arsène,
> à Magloire
> à Simon,
> à Simon,
> à Paul-Marie.
> That takes
> you back to the deportation.

> Paul-Marie was nine
> when it started
> at Beaubassin.
> My mother told me that.

He says this in the bemused tone
of someone who is surprised
to discover

he has become
an elder of the clan.

My father's hand slows
at a tall young man
standing at the back.
And I hear him say:
  That's Adolphus Deveau,
  the village vet.

Dad is now much older than Adolphus Deveau
and his voice
easily enters the photograph,
the soft sound of his Acadien accent
caught between the sepia grains, caught between memories,
the mysterious interstices
of time, life and death.
  Adolphus owned a small farm
  right next to the school.
  His apple trees
  bent down along the fenceline.
  His garden was
  a wild, disorganized place,
  overgrown with the remnants
  of old berry bushes
  and sprouting apple trees.
  Wild birds loved it,
  and limping,
  barnyard creatures everywhere,
  scratching chickens,
  rooting pigs,
  old, lazy, bandaged cats.
  The garden was in a warm dell,

with a little creek going by,
safe from the sea wind.
Sometimes
we broke the fenceline down
and Adolphus's pigs escaped.

Adolphus was a tall man,
well over six feet,
but took size seven shoes,
and when he chased his pigs,
he stumbled on his small feet,
falling to the ground
like a long, thin question mark,
the pigs squealing this way and that.
It was a funny thing to see.

My father stops talking,
remembering the old story
as if it is an ancient rhyme
from some old, old time,
yet he was the child
who had teased Deveau.

I smile at my dad
and between us
Adolphus Deveau comes
dancing down into the dining room,
down from the old sepia tones,
chasing his pigs on a cool,
Cape Breton morning.

Is there a photograph
like this in your house,
Henry?

Where your father's hand
passes slowly
along the rows of dark faces,
stopping at people
he remembers.

It seems miraculous.

I cannot see Adolphus Deveau,
the self-taught vet;
or Brigitte Aucoin, the jolly pauper;
or Wilfred à Marcellin,
the only verger in county Inverness;
or Magloire, my great-great-grandfather.

To me the faces all look the same,
blurred into similarity
by the dark tans and
old-fashioned clothes.
They could be Mi'kmaq people from Eskasoni
or Métis from Fort Carleton
dressed in their Sunday best
for the Bishop's visit.
They don't seem related to me.
I see only rows
of dark wool jackets that
pinch at the shoulders,
and women
in curious, voluminous dresses.

I need my father to guide me.

BATOCHE

Beyond the streets of Saskatoon,
the country rolls towards
the north.
It does not resemble
my image of the prairie.
It is too rounded with small hills,
and dotted by ponds.
It feels familiar.

We pass the Indian circle of the sun
at Wanuskewin.
All the while, the land
continues to rise
towards Batoche,
and we start to see
the old Métis fields outlined
along old fencelines by sumach and trees.
The fields are narrow as at Grand Étang,
running like fingers up from the river
past the shadows of houses and barns,
up to the back pastures.

I like them. They feel right.
The old Métis fields
are a sociable way to farm,
giving each family
their own road to the river,
giving each family
a fair slice of highlands and bottomlands.
Unlike square fields,
they turn farmers into villagers,
each country road into a country street,

lined by house and barn
each not far from the next,
each not far from the river.

At the graveyards of Batoche,
the river cliffs
plunge sharply down
to the water,
and across the river
the prairie wind
curls the long, silent grass
into sea waves.
It feels familiar
like the height of land
at Grand Étang and Chéticamp
where below the plateau the ocean curves
out towards the horizon.

It feels familiar,
as if I have been here before
and hunted on horseback,
as if I have ridden a small, tough pony,
driving buffalo towards the rock chutes,
feeling the wildness of pure exultation
in the thunder of hooves,
in the belly of the hunt.

It feels familiar,
as if there is nothing here
I do not know,
as if you and I have met before;
as if we have farmed together here;
as if we have harnessed the horses
and cut hay in the long July days,

the mowing machine whirring,
the blades cutting back and forth,
the horses' heads bowing
into their collars,
their legs straining;
streams of pungent sweat
soaking the harness, surrounded
by the sweet smell of the new grass
drying in the sun.

And near the house,
children tumble in the grass
like puppies in the spring sun
feeling the world
for the first time.

It feels to me
on this bright day,
as if this height of land,
this curve of river
have long been occupied;
as if at Batoche,
we are at the centre,
enfolding circle of life
where we have always been;
as if like willows by the river,
we have always been here,
and our roots have gone down hungrily
into the prairie earth,
and our leaves grown and drunk eagerly
from the sun;
as if we are eternal;
as if nothing has changed
and we are immortal;

as if there had been no war,
no deportation;
as if history had not happened.

You are a solitary painter
who sells his images
in the market.
And I a poet who struggles
to decipher the beat
of his own heart.

They have heard of you
in city shopping malls,
not at Batoche,
not here on this height of land,
populated only by graves and memories.

In Saskatoon,
I went looking for you
in the marketplace
among the sellers of knick-knacks
and home preserves,
but you had moved on.
And I drifted past the stalls
finding aprons and jams,
and wooden toys,
looking for Henry.

PRISONERS

It is a strange thing
to sit here
waiting for you,
waiting for someone
I have never met.

There is a book
in my hand with your paintings.
Louis Riel is here,
wearing his usual tight, dark, wool suit.
You have etched him
European style
into a stained glass window,
leaving him his dark brown eyes
with the mournful stare
of the Catholic saint
and the Cree elder.

Your book
rests in my hand
illuminated with your paintings
like an old Bible.
A jagged fenceline
of alder and birch
braided together
curls across the page.

They are good paintings.
You have found a way
to confront chaos
in your own life,
with nothing but paint and palette.

Sometimes, when I close
my eyes for sleep,

I see stones
floating
that have nothing,
that hold nothing,
that do not corrode,
that exist in emptiness,
with emptiness.

Has chaos won?
Does it always win?
Are your painting days finished?
Have you put
your palette down
and walked away?
Free to beg.
Free to drink.
Free to feel
the crack of eternity
across your own grave
and not care.

Maybe the stones
which I feel in my throat
are old injustices
which float from the past
to play games with us,
to press down on our souls in the night.

The souls of the defeated
are easy enough to see.
They stand on street corners,
hands out,
dressed in old clothes,

and exhausted faces.
Modern faces so much older
than the sepia tones
of old photographs
where men and women
stare confidently
out at me;
handsome men,
beautiful women,
balanced unknowing on the edge
of time's precipice.
A Cree man smokes a pipe.
His face dark
from the summer sun,
he sits confidently
in the stern of his canoe.
Strong, assured,
he wears
European clothes,
wool trousers,
a vest,
a linen shirt,
a broad-brimmed hat.
In front of him,
a dog sprawls sleeping
on a large, canvas bag.
He is going somewhere
because the canoe is packed
tightly from stem to stern.
But all the caption says is
         Guide, Red River, 1865.

A woman holds an infant,
its head peeking
out of the papoose cover.
The mother holds it
protectively to her chest.
She is tall and straight,
and beautiful
with wide-spaced eyes
and a perfect symmetry
of features.
The caption says,
      Squaw, Fort Garry, 1875.

The woman,
the man
are staring
right at me,
right through me.

Who are you?
They ask.
Who are you?

What if it is I
who am the prisoner?
I who must find the way
between the dots to them?

That the past and the future
collide in me, and
I am the prisoner.

They are elsewhere.

KNEELING

The stars make
cold companions.
I wish we could
see their children
playing in the starlight,
making their planetary circles
warmed by some foreign life.
But there is only
the hot moment
of our own candles
burning in the night;
burning in the words
of the people of Wanuskewin:
>        people
>        are no more than
>        a bird's shadow that flits
>        across the prairie grass at sunset.
>        No more than the warm breath
>        of bison on a cool morning.

These are brave words which
confront without crutch
the dismay of infinity and
the eternal round of beginnings and ends.

Braver than the God we imagine
and then run towards
like chicks to the hen
crying,
"Shelter me!
Protect me!
Hide me!
Give me the grace I cannot find!"

And when God hesitates,
we build monuments to our fears
and call them cathedrals.

## THE CHURCH OF ST. PIERRE

We have a great monument
in little Chéticamp.
A village cathedral
encrusted with fine wood carvings,
a church that testifies to our faith
in the shadow of the ocean,
on the edge of infinity.

It is just up from the harbour,
a great, ponderous brownstone building
with a tall spire
and spreading silver roof
that can be seen glinting in the sun
from Grand Étang to Cap Rouge.
It is bigger than the
old church at Grand Pré,
bigger than the crisped relic at Beaubassin.

And if God does not know the new one is there,
it is not our fault.
It is built from the same desires as
King Solomon's temple.

The last time
I was at St. Pierre,
I sat with Uncle Alex.
He is my father's eldest brother,
a firebrand of an old man
who still rages against
the injustice of the world.
As if justice
were the natural order of the universe
and we humans are too stupid
to grasp it,

as if, one day, we will.
Uncle Alex and Louis Riel
would s'entendent bien.

My Uncle Alex growls about the clergy,
growls about the congregation,
growls about the cost of churches
when people go hungry,
and comes to Mass each Sunday,
rain or shine, sleet or fair,
a rock in his faith.

I know very little.
That is mostly what I think
when I sit through
the old song of the Mass.

Waiting for the Mass to start,
The choirmaster plays
Pachelbel's Canon.
How beautiful the music is.
How curious that this universe bears
beautiful music and defeats men.
How arbitrary existence is.
It feels as if we are no more
than fish in the sea,
like two-legged cod herded into obedient,
predictable rows, heads bowed,
heads raised.
Helpless in our ambitions.
Devout in our cries.
Graceful in our songs.

I like the company of my uncle.
With or without his anger,

he has a sweet soul
and makes the day seem brighter
for being here.
Even in old age,
he has a richness about him,
a richness of human essentials.

His eldest son,
Marcel
was a great Cape Breton fiddler
and wrote a tune
before he died called
"Available Space".
A melody which haunts
with spaces and hesitations,
as if he knew his own timeline
was winding down.

From his youngest years,
he played
from Chéticamp to Hawkesbury.
He played with great insolence.
Never did anything else.
Just played the fiddle
wherever people wanted him.
Marcel never made any money.
Never married
Was the pride and despair of his family.
The doctors in Sydney told him
he had a bad heart
and needed an operation,
but it was not in Marcel's nature to worry.
After all
he was only forty-five.

Uncle Alex survived
the funeral of his eldest son
and of his wife, Annie.
He survived like old crystal, becoming
clearer and clearer,
brighter and brighter.

If Uncle Alex could wave a magic wand
there would be smiles where there is sadness,
generosity where there is meanness,
love where there is hatred,
and in the village,
a wide boardwalk
along the harbour
for lovers of all ages
to stroll
in the setting sun.

With another wave of his magic wand,
Marcel would not have died;
Aunt Annie would not
have gotten the nerve disease;
people would not grow old;
and he would not be addicted
to fancy shirts.

Uncle Alex cannot figure out
why richness of spirit and
pocketbook are not distributed
in equal measure.
At eighty, this still preoccupies him.
I figure it is because he has been
too close to both.
He has been a merchant all his life,

bought and sold things
up and down the coast,
first by horse and wagon,
then by car and truck,
then from a store.
This is a terrible thing,
for he has constantly seen
the best and worst in people.

The Mass begins.
The predictable comforting sounds
of the priest invoking
the presence of God.
The congregation sighs
and leans into its harness
beginning the heavy work
of laying down the metaphors
for the priest to walk on.

Uncle Alex and I sit together
in companionable silence.
Both of us sure
each in our own way
that there are angels,
and one day, their wings will catch us.

## VICTORY

There must be a
great and natural dissonance
among us humans.
Points where forces
we can't control collide,
and the human spirit cracks
like a rift valley
in the crust of the earth,
leaving mountains
on one side
and mountains on the other.

This must be what happens
when one man picks up a gun
and shoots another.
It is the crack not just
of a rifle,
but of the human spirit
into separate parts.

When I went running barefoot
across the soft prairie earth
that is what
I felt,
a great cracking
of the human spirit.
As if you and I had stumbled
into a rift
and it had exploded suddenly
into mountains around us.
You can see it
in the small round bullet holes
the soldiers have augured
like termite bites

in the clapboard steeple
of the church at Batoche.
Feel it
in the faint outlines
of the old fields and
the small,
obdurate gravestones
along the cliff.

Gervais,
Letendre,
Smith.
The gravestones tilt and yawn
like dull and fading windows
into a little time ago,
when the valley was different.
When there were great herds
of buffalo
and Assiniboine nomads
followed the wheel of the sun.

And then the crack
of the imperial rifle shot
and Gabriel Dumont's
tough little pony stumbles
down to the ground
a small piece of lead ripped
into his chest.

Dumont argues with his cousin,
trying to persuade him
to let his men fight
like ghosts in the night,
to harry and surprise,

not confront.
And Riel refuses,
determined to fight
soldiers like soldiers.
And like soldiers
the Métis charge up
the open hill
in front of their own village,
in front of their own kin,
where they fall like soldiers
before the Gatling gun.

And all I can feel
is a sundering
of the spirit
and the valley being formed.

We do it to ourselves.
Like water
eroding a hillside,
people erode each other.
Like water falling from the sky,
we feel obliged
to create dissonance
to carve valleys in the landscape
and then cry
for lost horizons.

It is we who create labels
like Métis and Acadien;
we who cut fields into the earth
and language into the minds,
to hold us together,

to tear us apart.
Half-breeds, Métis, Cajuns.
With our labels flying
we are blown across the land
like autumn leaves.

If young Riel could have
seen into the future,
seen his dark-suited body lying,
neck broken,
cemented silent
under a ton of brick and mortar
in the churchyard
of St. Boniface,
would he have done things differently?

If he could have heard
Queen Victoria intone sincerely
to the Empire on her
diamond jubilee,
    From my heart,
    I thank my beloved people.
    May God bless them.
Would he have done things differently?

Would he have still contended:
    You must understand
    there were two nations,
    one large and powerful,
    one smaller and less powerful,
    two unequal nations,
    but no less equal in rights.

And then the generals and colonels,
judges and juries
hanged him for a traitor.

"My Beloved People . . . "

LOOKING FOR HENRY    47

## MY BELOVED PEOPLE

Are you, Henry Letendre, related
to Leandre Letendre,
nicknamed Batoche,
the founder of Batoche,
in the same long way
la famille Doucet is
related to the date 1632
and Captain Germain Doucet
of Port Royal?

My own family tree
winds its way back through
Olivers and Hachés,
Landrys and LeBlancs,
Cormiers and Chiassons,
Boudreaus and Gallants,
Arseneaus and Melansons,
Robichauds and Therriaults,
past the Boston States,
past the New England factory jobs,
past the farms and fishing coves
of Cape Breton,
past the sea dikes,
past the orchards and saltwater meadows
of Grand Pré, Minas and Beaubassin
past Mi'kmaq and Acadien marriages
to 1632, Port Royal and
Captain Germain Doucet.

At Annapolis Royal,
you can find a book.
The book is in the guardhouse,
it notes the coming and going
of English soldiers.

There is a signature embalmed there,
a Lieutenant Doucet.
He is the duty officer on a July day, 1802.

The ink looks fresh,
the hand steady,
the signature testifies that
Lieutenant Doucet
has the right to carry a musket,
and wear the king's uniform;
that Lieutenant Doucet
has English manumission
to explode mountains
and bury valleys;
that the oath of allegiance
has been taken;
that the days of
"les français neutres",
that the days of old Acadie
are gone.

And so they were.

The militia arrived
and our narrow fields
were exploded into
the approved squares,
our villages burnt,
our dikes smashed,
our sea fields flooded,
our farms given away,
our Acadie renamed,
and our people thrown upon the sea
like so many grains of old seed,

like the Métis at Batoche
before the approved order
of Queen and colonels.

"My beloved people."

## MY GRANDFATHER'S HOUSE

There were no books in my grandfather's house.
There was no time to read.
A small farm and ten children
takes the edge off the printed page.
Besides, Grandpapa could not read.
He had been busy ever since he could remember, working.
Smart children worked.
Nor was there national rancour
in my grandfather's house.
Grandpapa could have met Queen Victoria
if she had passed by
and said to her,
"Pleased to meet you, Ma'am.  May I introduce my grandson."
And her small hand would have entirely disappeared
like a child's into his large one.
And when I stumbled
avec une phrase maladroite,
il m'aurait dit,
— N'aie pas peur, Clive,
Notre français est bon.
He understood the territories of beloved
were grand and moved upon them easily
and in his way, in this way, without books,
taught me.

*Part II*
*Billet Acadien*

When I was twelve, my parents put me on a plane in Ottawa and sent me to spend the summer at my grandfather Doucet's. He lived in the small village of Grand Étang, near the northeast tip of Cape Breton Island. I spoke no French. The village was entirely French-speaking and entirely Acadien. It was as if, when I crossed the bridge at Margaree Harbour, I had entered another country, yet I needed no passport to enter it. I needed nothing more than to be Clive à Fernand, à William, à Arsène. Clive the son of Fernand, the son of William, the son of Arsène, and people would know where I lived and why I belonged in the rough country of les terres hautes de Cape Breton.

I lived in the white house with the red barn behind it, about a mile from the harbour. What I did not know, and took many years to understand, was that my father was born in this village, and my grandfather before him, because of something called "la déporta-tion". That my grandfather's antique French, the poverty and isola-tion of our village, the need to go away to be educated and find work as my father had done, all began in 1755. In that year on August 11, in the village of Beaubassin on the lush, flat marshlands at the head of the Bay of Fundy, an eight-year-old boy named Paul-Marie Doucet somehow missed being rounded up by the soldiers and put on British ships as were his parents, brothers and sisters. Instead, he escaped into the woods where he lived with the Mi'kmaq people until, eventually, he, his wife Félicité-Michel, and their three boys would find their way to the isolated shores of Cape Breton.

My grandfather, five generations on, was connected to the vast convulsion of "la déportation" just by being who he was. I don't believe he ever left Cape Breton Island. When I went to the farm that first summer he was in his early seventies. We spent each day together from milking in the early morning to splitting wood at the woodpile at the end of the day. Grandpapa wasn't so much a storyteller as someone who just recounted the things that had happened to him. He had arrived at that stage in life when, I think, although neither of us realised it, he was instinctively passing things on that were important to him. And there was no better place to listen to a story than by the woodpile in the early evening, the sun setting behind the sea, soft sound of summer around us, as we slowly finished the last chore of the day.

The stories were always connected to Acadie because that was what Grandpapa knew. Some were stories about the battles between the priest and the young men who wanted to organise the great Chandeleur party. The Chandeleur masqueraded as one of the church's holy festivals, and there was a Chandeleur Mass on Sunday with a blessing of the Chandeleur candles by the priest, but in fact it was a festival as pagan as the Mardi Gras, and if it became too wild, the priest could threaten to close it down by refusing to bless the candles.

The young men, my grandfather among them, would "run the Chandeleur", galloping happily across the fields by sleigh from house to house collecting the food and drink for the great party, and in thanks would sing the traditional song, "l'Escaouette".

I can remember Grandpapa singing the song of "l'Escaouette," and dancing, pretending he was young, wishing he were young, disbelieving that all the years could have passed by; that he could have buried two dearly-loved wives and seen his many children grow up and leave. How did such things happen so quickly? So finally?

GOVERNOR BLUES

"It appears to me that you think yourselves
independent of any government and
you wish to treat with the King
as if you were so."

> *Governor Edward Cornwallis to Acadien delegates in 1749*

## AS IF YOU WERE SO

There were these mornings.
There were these music lessons.
There were these evenings.
There were these plays.
There were these days.
There were these wigs
and gentlemen at court.
There were these armies.
There were these fortresses.
There were these walled cities.

There was this
King Capet encore.
There was this
Cardinal Richelieu,dressed in red.
There was this
war against the Huguenots.
There was this
Malade imaginaire.
There was this
Diderot who compiled.

Across the sea,
in another place,
there were these mornings.
Across the sea,
there were other days.
Across the sea,
there were other ways.

There was this young woman named Evangeline
There was this young man named Gabriel
Who cared nothing for courts and kings

And Malades imaginaires,
Who rose with the morning sun,
Whose world was composed differently.

## DINNER AT FORT BEAUSÉJOUR

The nights are often
of a startling clarity
at Beaubassin.
On the marshes,
the sea and sky blend
into a common web
and the summer evening
lulls soldier and Acadien alike.

A good place
for a quiet dinner
in the new house
of Commander de Vergor.
A good place to contemplate
the Acadien barns which dot the marshes
like boats moving slowly
on the sea.
A good place
for lamb stew and cider,
apple pie and cream.
From the windows of the house,
you can contemplate
the stately turn of earth
among the stars.

A good place for Colonels
Monckton, Scott and Winslow
to savour their victory,
and for de Vergor
to consider the career
possibilities of defeat.

In the distance,
Abbé Le Loutre's new church
still smoulders,

sending a long, thin tendril
of acrid smoke
into the evening sky.
Torched by the Abbé himself,
who would rather have it burned
by the good Catholic hands that built it,
than suffer otherwise,
before he returned to Québec,
sans soutane.

Oh, it was not
a happy meal
that 16th day of June, 1755.
The Boston militia
complain the English
take credit for everything
and do little.
The English
complain the Boston militia
confuse deer hunting
with the business of war.
The French
complain the Acadiens
were reluctant to shoot redcoats.
The Acadiens
complain their oath of neutrality
has been compromised by the French.
And Commander de Vergor
is stuck eating apple pie
in his own house,
staring at his own Beaubassin sky,
conversing with the victors
under the guns
of defeat.

## AUGUST 11, 1755

" . . . that your Lands & Tenements,
Cattle of all Kinds and Live Stock
of all Sortes are Forfitted
to the Crown
with all other your Effects Saving
your Money & Household goods
and you yourselves to be removed from
this his province."

*Lieutenant-Colonel John Winslow,*
*read first at Beaubassin, summer, 1755*

There was this day
which was beautiful.
There was this morning
when the sun rose
above the horizon,
above the sea,
above the road,
above the trees
and the north country
was suffused
with the colours of the rainbow,
with all the promise
that is or was possible.
And on this day,
each creature of the earth
felt blessed and easy.
Humanity, for a moment,
was redeemed.
There was no plan
to this day.
No holy sacrament.
No computer.

No army.
No government.
Like the valleys
being formed.
Like the mountains
being raised,
it just happened.
It was a cruel day.
A day when accomplishment
evaporated.
A day for burning poems
and living, content,
in the interstices
of God.

## There Were Always Birds

There were always birds
upon the marshes.
The sounds chattering in the air
like the conversation of angels.
In the spring, they would arrive
flying from the south in clouds
that laid a shadow between earth
and sun.

The Mi'kmaq people said the marsh
was the place where the world began.

The boy's home
was along the height of land
where Acadien houses were strung
like beads between the marshes
and the hills.
The boy's memory of that time
came and went in jagged flashes
as in a dream.

There was a kitchen in the dream,
an uncle, a fireplace, a table,
black pots hanging beside the fireplace.

Sometimes there was music
and in the eye of the music
his mother danced.

The uncle winked,
a small conspiracy.

The boy was lying on the dike
the grass soft against his stomach.
He was gazing down into the water

waiting for the tide
to creak the clapets closed,
sealing the fields safely from the sea
the creak of the hinges
jangling in the dream.

Sometimes, he was lying lazily on his side,
surrounded by the scents of summer flowers,
watching the grass bend in the field,
the ships out in the bay,
their sails billowing in the wind
like earthly clouds.

Sometimes, he was fishing.
The Mi'kmaq language around him,
sounding sweet
like the stream eddying
at his feet.

Sometimes,
he was on his father's shoulders
and they were walking across the fields
towards the horizon.

The boy was tired and slept long.
Unaware of the year, of the date,
of the approach of the king's men,
of the demise of old regimes,
and the gestation of wars
among nations.

He was just a boy with memories
barely formed.

When he awoke,

he smelt something different,
not the pleasant scent of wood fire
burning in the stove,
something more acrid,
something more bitter,
and the boy stood up slowly,
his eyes gummed
with too deep a sleep.

Along the ridge,
columns of dark smoke
rose towards the sky.

His house was burning.

The boy began to run
towards the house
crying Mama! Papa!
Summer dreams forgotten.

But there was no one home.
No Mama.
No Papa.
No Brothers.
No Sisters.

The boy was alone in the yard beside the house.
His mother's sunflowers smiling,
The snap of walls buckling,
the hay in the yard flaring
in great sheets of orange flame,
the heat making the boy sweat.

Mama! Papa!
But they were gone,
and his voice melted unheard
into the roar of the fires.

BILLET ACADIEN: ALLER ÉVANGÉLINE
COMPOSTÉ AUGUST, 1755

(*from* Evangeline *by Longfellow*)

Half way down the shore Evangeline waited in
        silence,
Not overcome with grief, but strong in the hour of
        affliction,
Calmly, sadly, she waited, until the procession
        approached her,
And she beheld the face of Gabriel pale with emotion,
Tears filled her eyes, and, eagerly running to meet
        him,
Clasped she his hands, and laid her head on his
        shoulder, and whispered, —
"Gabriel! Be of good cheer! For if we love one another,
Nothing, in truth, can harm us, whatever mischances
        may happen!"

    Beaubassin, August 15, 1755
    to Europe

    Grand Pré, September 1755
    to Massachusetts

    Port Royal
    1755 to
    Connecticut

    Beaubassin
    1755 to New York

    Beaubassin
    1755 to Maryland

Smiling she spake these words; then suddenly paused,
        for her father

Saw she slowly advancing.  Alas! How changed was his
      aspect!
Gone was the glow from his cheek, and the fire from his
      eye, and his footstep
Heavier seemed the weight of the heavy heart in
      his bosom.
But, with a smile and a sigh, she clasped his neck and
      embraced him,
Speaking words not of endearment where words of comfort
      availed not.

    Cobequid
    1755-7 to
    England

    Minas
    1755 to
    South Carolina

    La rivière aux Canards
    1755 to
    North Carolina

Thus to the Gaspereau's mouth moved on that
      mournful procession.
There disorder prevailed, and the tumult and stir of
      embarking.
Busily plied the freighted boats; and in the confusion
Wives were torn from their husbands, and mothers, too
      late, saw their children
Left on the land, extending their arms, with wildest
      entreaties.
So unto separate ships were Basil and Gabriel carried,
While in despair on the shore Evangeline stood with
      her father.

Half the task was not done when the sun went down,
     and the twilight
Deepened and darkened around; and in the haste the
     refluent ocean
Fled away from the shore, and left the line of the sand-
     beach
Covered with waifs of the tide, with kelp and the
     slippery sea-weed.

    Piziquid
    1755 to
    Georgia

    Piziquid
    1758-60 to
    France

    Minas
    1755 to
    France

    Isle St. Jean
    1763-1766 to
    France

    Falklands
    1769-75 to
    France

    the ship Violet from France
    1758 to
    bottom of the sea

Farther back in the midst of household goods and
     the wagons,

Lay encamped for the night the houseless Acadian
      farmers.
Back to its nethermost caves retreated the bellowing
      ocean,
Dragging adown the beach the rattling pebbles, and
      leaving
Inland and far up the shore the stranded boats of the
      sailors.
Then, as the night descended, the herds returned from
      their pastures;
Sweet was the moist still air with the odour of milk
      from their udders;
Lowering they waited, and long, at the well-known bars
      of the farmyard,

    France
    1764 to
    Saint Dominique

    Halifax
    1763 to
    Cayenne

    Cap Sable
    1763 to
    Massachusetts,

    Acadie
    St. Pierre et Miquelon
    Acadie (date not clear)

    Les îsles de la Madeleine,
    1765 to
    Acadie

Waited and looked in vain for the voice and the hand of
      the milkmaid.
Silence reigned in the street; from the church no
        Angelus sounded,
Rose no smoke from the roofs, and gleamed no lights
      from the windows.

    Rémshic
    Restigouche
    Halifax
    Rémshic, encore
    Louisbourg
    Isle St. Jean
    Québec
    Martinique

        et d'autres endroits

GABRIEL

Who were you Gabriel?
Always on the run,
driven from town to town,
from forest to river
from place to place.

Who were you?
Peering over the railing.
The hot August sun
on your back.
Watching columns of fire
rising from the village.
The mountain patched
with flame.

Who were you?
Turning to watch the soldiers
holding their guns.
Your fists balled
in trouser pockets
until the nails went numb.

Who were you, Gabriel?
Who felt his tomorrows
slowly crumble into age
without a yesterday.

Were you the kind of hero
who could not read,
who could not write,
yet could put his shoulder
against the wheel of life
and slow its roll?

Were you the kind of man
to raise ten children
in a little salt box house
and keep the flint in your soul
for warming others?

Were you the kind of man
to love recklessly, forever?

THERE IS THIS QUESTION

There is the idea
of France
which hangs
about the necks
of Frenchmen
like Sioux war beads.
A heavy necklace
of photographs and words
marked
Place de la Concorde,
Pont Neuf,
Café du coin,
Le Tour de France,
Le baiser de l'Hotel de ville,
Les Fleurs du mal,
Chateau, village
and accent.

There is the question
of Acadie without war beads.

There is the question
of walking,
of walking
without the war beads,
without the necklace,
without the images
marked home.
There is the question
of walking.

There
is the question
of self-esteem

which hangs
like a fragile necklace
around our necks.
In the pearl necklace
of the tight-lipped lady
dressed for church;
in the bone embroideries
of Sioux warriors
dressed for war;
in the paintbrush
of Henry Letendre.
And in the lost voice
of Grandmother No-name
which survives behind
the pearl necklace,
the bone embroideries,
the paintbrush of Henry Letendre,
in the echo of the universe.

L'ESCAOUETTE

The exile is branded here.
Not in *Evangeline*.
Burnt here in the song of l'Escaouette.

> C'est monsieur l'marié et madam' marié
> C'est monsieur, madam' mariés
> Qu'ont pas encor soupé.
> Un p'tit moulin sur la rivière,
> Un p'tit moulin pour passer l'eau.
> Le feu sur la mountain, boy run, boy run,
> Le feu sur la mountain, boy run away.
> J'ai vu le loup, le r'nard, le lièvre,
> J'ai vu la grand' cité sauter,
> J'ai foulé ma couvert',couvert', vert', vert'.
> J'ai foulé ma couvert',couverte aux pieds.
>
> Aouenne, aouenne, aouenne, nippaillon!
> Ah! rescou' tes brillons.
> Tibounich, nabet, nabette!
> Tibounich, naba!

PLACES

A man writes
laboriously,
slowly,
humbly
to a New England authority
requesting permission
to move from one town to another:

> Can I please move to New Haven?
> For I have found a sister there
> and she is the only
> relative I have been able to find.

The helplessness of the brother
is amazing.

A proud man
writing simply,
in a strange language,
asking for a small freedom.

The eviscerating pain of Evangeline
is embalmed there.
Not in the romance of,
"This is the forest primeval; the murmuring pines and the
      hemlocks."

I never understood the poem.

My picture of Acadie
was always high bluffs over a cold sea,
mountains crowding the farms,
eagles screaming from treetops.
This was my Acadie.
The Acadie of mountain pastures,

fish flakes,
little coves,
and long horizons.

A hard place
to gain a living,
where the land gives up its children
easily,
where farmers till thin soil
between the spring break of shore ice
and the onset of autumn storms
which hammer upon the coast,
daring men to walk straight.
And parents prepare their
children from birth for flight.

"Where is the thatch roofed village, the home of the Acadian
farmers, —
Men whose lives glided on like the rivers that water the wood-
lands,"
writes Longfellow.

Chéticamp is as far from
the valley of Evangeline
as the shack side of the Edmonton tracks
is from the village of Batoche.

The valley of Evangeline
was southern,
sheltered from the rude Atlantic,
in a gentle arc of land
around a wide bay,
where the soil is a deep, reddish brown
and spreading hardwoods line the roads,
where seeds grow by common accord

of sun and earth,
and the breeze bends gently
across the dark fields of corn,
that was the Acadie of Evangeline,
not little Chéticamp
hidden beneath the dark mountains.

BILLET ACADIEN — RETOUR PELAGIE

### 1765

à

Taguenich, P.E.I.

Rusticot, P.E.I.

Malpèque, P.E.I.

Casconpec, P.E.I.

Rivière des Blancs, P.E.I.

### 1770

Bedéque, P.E.I.

Chéticamp, N.S.

Magré, N.S.

Grand Étang, N.S.

Mission Sainte-Maire, N.S.

Grande Digue, N.S.    D'Escousse, N.S.

Arichat, N.S.

### 1774

L'Ardoise, N.S.

Rivière à Bourgeois, N.S.

Havre-à-Boucher, N.S.

Pommequette, N.S.

Tracadie, N.S.

Haut-de-Tousket, N.S.

Milieu-de-Touskuet, N.S.

### 1777

Bas-de-Touskuet, N.S.                     Pobomcoup, N.S.

Mission Saint Anne, N.B.

Petitcodiac, N.B.

Memramcook, N.B.

Gédiaque, N.B.
Barachois, N.B.

Cocagne, N.B.

1778
Bouctouche, N.B.
Richiboutou, N.B.
Chigibougouachiche, N.B.
Chigibougonet, N.B.
Baie-des-Winds, N.B.

1780
La Haute Pointe, N.B
Tabusintac, N.B.
Tracadie, N.B.
Pokemouche, N. B.
Chipâgan, N.B.          Caraquet, N.B.

1782
Nepisiguit, N.B.          Petit Rocher, N.B.
Ardoine, N.B.          Rivière à Jaquet, N.B.
Mission de Madawaska, N.B.

1783

Louisiana

Louisiana

Louisiana
Billet Acadien: Aller et Retour, 18 years

## LA PÊCHE À LA BALEINE

Along the cliffs
an eagle spirals
slowly upwards,
its wings spread
like sails in the evening sun.
Its shadow
a dark stain
moving across the cliff face,
like a puff of God,
impenetrable,
obdurate,
powerful,
evanescent.

Below the cliffs,
my cousins hunt whales,
three times a day,
the boats go out
loaded with tourists
and cameras.
All hungry to record
on celluloid,
the monsters which
rise like houses
from the sea
to breathe.

My grandfather's barn
was painted
with whale oil fat
and red vegetable dye;
and on hot summer days,
the barn sailed
back to the sea.

The whale's corpse was spread
from barn to corset,
to medicine,
to pig pen,
to bone meal
for the garden.

Whales, seals, swordfish,
cod, halibut, flounder,
mackeral, smelts,
lobster, crab,
trout, salmon,
moose, deer, rabbit,
cows, pigs, sheep,
chickens, plants
of every description,
there was nothing
that was safe
from the plate.

Now, we buy food wrapped
in plastic;
take pictures
of the whales
and tell people
about the bad old days
when people
were acquainted
with lunch.

Along the cliffs,
an eagle glides
slowly upwards.
A fish in its claws,
its shadow
like a stain
against the rock.

## CHANSON ACADIENNE

Le monde de Chatican
Travaillons à la turn
Et les moineaux pareillement.
William à Arsène qu'est boss.
Tout le monde s'en trouve bien.
Pierre à Dominique cook.
Nous l'faut absolument,
Et p'tit Thommy qui marque le temps.

This song is from the 1930s
in the days of the Great Depression
when there was no money,
and people lived
close to the land,
close to the sea,
close to each other.

The highland trails
were built during these days
by crews of men,
paid by the government
to put some money into the pockets
of the people who had none.
The men lived in solitary work camps
along the rivers
and valleys of the park.

I remember my grandfather
recounting how they built them
with nothing
but picks and shovels,
horses and carts.
Trails up into the highlands
to the waterfalls

and lakes,
to the old hunting grounds
of the Mi'kmaq.
Trails for tourists
from away.

He was proud of them
and would be pleased to know
they're still there.
They were his dikes
against the sea,
his harbingers
of good times
and he pressed his men
to build them
the best way they could.
So that they drained well
and the footbridges curved
across the streams
safe and strong.

William à Arsène
was the first Acadien
in my family
to become Canadian.
The first to vote
and believe Canada
was a good thing.

> Oh! venez pour entendre chanter
> Ca c'que j'ai composé
> Après l'ouvrage à la veillée.

C'est en égard d'l'ouvrage
Qui s'fait dans Chatican,
Ä proos d'un parc,
Vous le savez fort bien.
Ca paiera-t-il? On n'en sait rien.

## LES GRANDMÈRES SANS NOMS

A young woman
stands in the clearing
near the gate of Port Royal.
She is with some friends.
She is beautiful.
I can see her plainly enough.
Seventeen? Eighteen?
Dressed in deerskin.
And then the image fades.
Her face is dark.
Eyes luminous brown circles,
she waves to me
from such a long, long way.

Oh, I would like to meet her,
to hear the sound of her voice,
to know her name,
to speak together.
She is my Mi'kmaq grandmother.
From her I descend.
From her I arrive.
Grandmother No-name,
Our line of la famille Doucet
is descended from her and Pierre Doucet,
son of Germain.

She died young, leaving one young son
and a husband who grieved.
There are no pictures, no songs,
no mother tongue,
not even a family name;

Mi'kmaq grandmothers being recorded
by first name and a blank space.
　　　Margarite _____,
　　　Femme de Pierre,
the blank space echoing with
Mi'kmaq uncles and aunts,
cousins and cousines disappearing
into an empty line
that echoes on the soul's drum.

In my dreams, there is a girl
standing by the dance hall door
at Eskasoni, down the coast from Grand Étang.
She is beautiful
with soft, brown eyes
that are neither sad nor happy.
She is hesitating at the door,
talking with a friend,
looking to dance inside.
I stand young and helpless
before her soft fire,
tongue-tied, dumb;
too many years of the world
cutting at the connections between us.
It is easier to reach
for a beer,
to slow the spinning of the planet,
to forget that a slice of my own soul
has gone missing.

In my dreams,
I know my grandmother's name.

In my dreams,
she is a girl laughing.
In my dreams,
she is a young woman
with three sons
who tumble about her long skirt.

In my dreams,
she is an old woman
sitting on the shore,
her legs sprawled comfortably,
splitting salmon with strong, easy strokes.
Her hair is still black.
And she looks into my brown eyes
and we smile
rich as a long summer's day,
rich as the stars which light our way.

## THERE'S A HILL

There's a hill
at the back
of our farm.
On one side
is the saltwater pond
after which
the village is named.
On the other,
you can see
up and down
the rough coastline
that the Doucets
and the Cormiers,
Hachés and Leblancs,
Chiassons and Deveaus,
Aucoins and Poiriers,
Leforts and Leverts
have occupied
since 1780.
It can be beautiful.
The sea limpid,
the mountains verdant
and billowing with colour.
And it can be wild
and buffeted by gales.

My friend Gérard à Levis
and I are walking
across the fields
to his house.
It is high summer
and the evening sun

is warm.
I am happy
to be with my friend.

Down the coastline,
I can see the spire
of St. Pierre
at Chéticamp.

My Uncle Alex
and Aunt Annie
live there,
where they have
a store
at the entrance
of the village.

Uncle Philias,
the schoolteacher,
and Aunt Catherine
live at the other end
by the harbour mouth.
The Doucets bracketing the village
like bookends.

In the music
of my summer days,
I can hear Marcel.
He is already becoming famous.
At ten, he plays
at dances.
People already
know his name.
No one needs to say
Marcel à Alex à William,

his name stands by itself.
Marcel Doucet will do.
The boy who could
play the fiddle
at three.

From the hill
at the back of the farm,
I can pick out
the houses and barns
of my family.

Uncle Gérard
and Aunt Lucy-Mae's
big white house in the centre of the village.
Grandpapa's smaller house
on the rising land towards the mountains,
the fields around it green.
Magah's house,
crumbling like a wrecked ship
sur la butte.

In this small, stark
corner of the world
are the houses and songs,
laughter and love
of the people
who are of me
and I of them.

People
are no longer fastened
to the landscape
in the same way.

People
are learning
to be people
without acres and homesteads
attached to them
like umbilical cords.

But I am glad that I had the chance
to touch the old ways
and feel
the turning of the village earth
like an old lady
drunk with happiness.

PART III
MÉTIS TICKET

I remember Louis Riel, the Métis leader, being described as unstable, a religious fanatic who had blocked the expansion of Canada westwards. He was hung for treason because of his participation in the Métis rebellion of 1885. That's all I remember from my high school history classes and all that really stuck with me over the years until I visited Batoche with Glen Sorestad.

The Métis were no more than caricatures in my head, half-Indian, half-White, chasing buffalo across the plains before being, unfortunately, necessarily, suppressed so that the West could be settled by farmers. It never occurred to me for a moment that they, like the Acadiens, were a people; that they farmed the land as my ancestors had; that on Sunday, in villages like Batoche, they went to little, white clapboard churches as we did in Grand Étang. It never occurred to me that they were English-speaking as well as French- and Cree-speaking; that they were a complex, original people who had developed linked villages and a sense of themselves as a nation able to govern themselves and negotiate with other nations.

Nor did it occur to me to question the gospel received from my teachers that Sir John A. Macdonald was a statesman, and Louis Riel an unfortunate rebel. I didn't know anything about Riel's Bill of Rights or that Thomas Scott, the Protestant, was not lynched but received a jury trial with a distinguished defence lawyer acting on his behalf. I didn't know anything about the $5,000 bounty placed on Riel's head after his government was suppressed by force or how he was hounded across the 49th parallel and worn down by years on the run.

I didn't know that the Loyal Orange Lodge, which remains one of the most divisive and violent organizations ever to grace the human condition, had captured the ear and the political conviction of Sir John A. That the suppression of the Métis had as much to do with ethnic and religious violence as anything else.

When I visited Batoche, I understood for the first time the connections between the Acadien and Métis people and the grinding reality of displacing and disconnecting people from their homes, villages and farms. This endures much longer than any words on a page. While I was at Batoche, I met a Métis man who had brought his grandson over from Edmonton and was telling him about the last battle of the Métis. The lives of the Métis people, like the lives of Acadiens, continue to be shadowed by the events which emptied their communities and ended a way of life.

LOOKING

I have telephoned art galleries
and curators have given me
the dates of your flourishing.
And I have learned artists
are classified
as if they were flowers
with their bloom dates noted.

WALKING

It is explained
that you were born
in Fort Chipewyan.
They know of you
in Saskatoon.
You have sold
many paintings there.
I have a fading, newspaper clipping
from 1984.
Your existence
is accounted
in your paintings.
Your disappearance
as natural.
"Artists are free spirits,"
they tell me.
They come and go.
I listen
and am not so sure.
Most artists
I know
have ferocious attachments,
to people, to islands,
to cities, to coastlines,
to mountains.
Their roots push down
like pernicious weeds,
seeking some hold
in the earth's crust
against the solar wind.

Where are you?
I write to a village
in Saskatchewan

where I am told
you have blown.
But the letter
is returned unopened.
I can feel
the solar wind
and the stamp of buffalo
on a cold morning.

## A WOMAN FROM WINNIPEG

A woman from Winnipeg
heard me on the radio
and sent me
a colour photo
of a painting
she bought
in 1968.
It is of a figure,
leaning
out a window;
the figure
is suffused
in pale, winter sunlight,
and in the bottom corner
the scrawl Letendre.

The woman from Winnipeg wrote,
"this painting has often comforted me.
I bought it for next to nothing when I had next to nothing."

LOOKING

I bought a painting
by a Mi'kmaq painter
in Big Cove,
hoping it
would bring me the luck
of good things.

## FROM AWAY

God's rules don't seem
to include staying put.
As often as not,
people tumble about
the planet's surface.
Looking for a toehold.
Riel was always
on the run
from something.
The enemies of Riel
were "from away".
From Orange Ontario.

From away, a good down-home
expression
which means
the ether of existence
beyond Cape Breton.

In Moncton,
"from away"
is more specific.
It means from Montréal,
New England,
Louisiana,
France.
And carries the label
"run away".
Not always friendly.
From away.

Riel won a scholarship
and was sent away at fourteen

to study in Montréal,
spent most of his adolescent life away
before coming home,
before being sent away
permanently at forty.

Yet, he packed
so much in his life:
Cree, Assiniboian,
French, English,
Latin, Greek.
Travels.
Poems.
Speeches.
Prayers.
Teaching.
Preaching.
Hunting.
Farming.
Great loves.
Great despair.
Great hope.
There is no hero
of his stripe in Acadie.
No one who could frighten
the politicians and colonels,
bishops and soldiers
with words.

RED RIVER

Is Fort Chipewyan
like Grand Étang?
One of those forgotten places
where our people washed up
after the deportation?
After Red River?
After Batoche?

It sounds like an old Bay trading post
with Chipewyan people camped nearby.
I see it
in my mind's eye
a scattering of houses
against a northern sky.
I see it like Grand Étang
buried in the Cape Breton highlands.
Distant from the memories
of militia and smoke columns rising
along the shore;
distant from young men
striding across the prairie
in buckskin and bravado
to confront
the Queen's surveyors.
Young Louis Riel at their head,
raises
his hand dramatically — palm outward,
his dark curly hair
framing a pale face,
his voice
crisp and clear:

"You go no farther."

There are no guns.
Just words.

"You go no farther.
This land belongs to Monsieur Marion."

The words echo between the men
like wolves
pissing out their boundaries.

Our land at the Red River
and the Assiniboine.
Our buffalo that tread the earth.
Our eagles that coast in the sky.
Our cattle that graze in the fields.
Ours because we were here first.
Ours because we have befriended
the land and it has befriended us.

The surveyors argue,
no-one owns anything
until the land has been
divided into square sections
that will sit properly in the
imperial cake pan
"for the appropriate settlers."
Except these last words are left unsaid.

But the Métis boys hear
what is left unsaid,
and do not want their narrow fields
changed into square sections,
do not want to be dispossessed
for appropriate settlers.

And they will not move.
The young man named Riel
repeats obdurately:

"You go no farther."

The words are
meant for the surveyors,
but the voice that says them
carries half way round the world.
The imperial machine
has run into a rock.
Louis Riel has taken
his place in the valley
for the rifting
of humanity
into the old zones
marked included
and excluded.

The surveyors grow impatient.
Half-breeds do not dictate terms.
Half-breeds do as they are told
and disappear mutely further north
into the appropriate fold of the earth.

This land is to be painted into
into golden posters
and advertised in post offices
and railway stations,
in Canada, in Europe
with men, holding sheaves of wheat,
glowing in the sun
and women with chubby,

healthy babies.
And on the golden poster
people are exhorted to:
"Come west and homestead!"

But the Métis would not move
and the imperial tailors
picked up their notebooks
and plumb lines,
stakes and chains
leaving
the wrinkle of Riel
in the landscape;
leaving the young men victors
on the open field;
leaving colonels and Gatling gun
to sort it out.

WALKING

Although the world
is not fair,
it is supposed to be.

The world is divided
between those like my Uncle Alex
who believe this to be so,
and those who think him a fool.
For the world is not fair
and cannot be.
Therefore be sensible,
accept the logic of the winning side.
Louis Riel
fell into the circle
of fools.
And the world
defeated him,
leaving him
like my Uncle
to pray to God,
who is never fair,
who is never unfair,
who is just there.

A river of Masses,
a river of prayers
poured forth from Louis Riel.
Even labelled insane,
and bottled away,
he went faithfully
to Mass each day,
sometimes twice,

as he tried to understand
what had gone wrong,
why there was a price
on his head
and assassins
at the door.

LOOKING

I have been
interviewed
on the radio
and had to explain
in the rawness of sound
that you have become
a metaphor
for looking for myself,
for looking for Acadie,
for looking for the past
that was of our grandfathers,
that was of ourselves,
but not written.

## THOMAS SCOTT

CRACK! CRACK! CRACK!
The shots rang out
and Thomas Scott,
Protestant,
jumped and slumped
before the firing squad,
pearly alcohol
in the firing squad,
pearly blood at the feet
of the Irish Orangeman.

These things happen.
Scott detested half-breeds.
He couldn't help it.
Scott detested
a great deal.
He detested that
he was not rich
enough, quick enough.
He detested
that the world had Catholics;
that there were bosses;
that there were half-breeds;
he detested that he had to wake
each morning
and find his face
still nailed
sullenly in place.
He was that kind
of man.
The solar wind
scratches at the throat
and people cough
up gobs of hate.

It seems natural
enough.
Bile collects.

You can't say the Métis
were innocent.
They put the Orangeman's finger
on the imperial trigger
by shooting Thomas Scott,
by resisting
made-in-England civilization
and exported to Canada
like so many red Toyotas,
like so many *Die Hard* videos,
by so many aides-de-camp.

These things happen.
Two dead in fair exchange,
a third by firing squad
is small European change
in the rifting of nations.

These things happen.
Rainforests are burnt.
Shots fired.
Women raped.
Men shot.

CRACK! CRACK! CRACK!
Thomas Scott
jumps and slumps
before a firing squad.
His blood nothing more
than an hors d'oeuvre.

## FANG HISTORY

Thomas Scott tried, convicted
and shot for treason.
So what?
He was disreputable, dangerous.

The young president acquiesced to the death,
busy as only a young man
can be,
busy knitting together
the geography of a new government,
an elected assembly,
new laws,
letters to Ottawa and London,
busy patching together
a Bill of Rights
and European legality
for the Métis.
He did not stop to understand
what disaster had befallen him;
didn't realize
that it was not the fairness of the trial
that counted,
that it did not matter
that Scott was violent, dangerous,
and left unattended,
collected acrid sores about him;
did not comprehend
it was the symbol
of the firing squad
which was the affront.

Helpless, hapless Thomas Scott,
PROTESTANT! PROTESTANT, PROTESTANT!
tied up and disposed of

like so much unwanted baggage.
The story of his execution would rage
across Orange Ontario as
Métis savages on the loose;
as the half-breed, half-civilized,
rabbit-reproducing Catholic
versus the sturdy and worthy Thomas Scott, Protestant.

At Queen's Park,
the colonels and majors,
captains and lieutenants,
sergeants and corporals,
fathers and sons
gathered,
swollen in their itchy uniforms
drawn like August horseflies
towards hot, juicy sweat.
For Thomas Scott was shot in the days
when the Catholic and Protestant
marquees were glittering with
mutual, visceral distaste.

I am boring you, Henry.
I can feel it myself
in the clammy familiars
of old metaphors
and ethnic cleansing.
I understand.
It is such an old refrain:

Protestant
          vs Catholic

Catholic
          vs Protestant

Serbian
      vs Croatian

Muslim
      vs Christian

Sikh
      vs Hindu

Hindu
      vs Muslim

Mayan
      vs Mexican

Armenian
      vs Turk

Zulu
      vs Xhosa

ANC
      vs Ikantha

Palestinian
      vs Jew

White
      vs Black

Boer
      vs British

Chinese
      vs Japanese

Eritrean
      vs Ethiopian

Somalian
      vs Somalian

French
> vs English

Latvian
> vs Russian

Pole
> vs German

Basque
> vs Spaniard

Tamil
> vs Sinhalese

Indonesian
> vs East Timorese

Hutu
> vs Tutsi

and
Amazon Indians
> vs the World.

So it goes.
Shots are fired.
Rainforests burnt.
Women raped.
Voices
buried in cannon shot,
leaving lives
like the sweet memories
of a spring day.
People gutted like fish
and left to rot
on the shore.

These things happen.
We inherit these wounds
from the fang history of man
to bleed each generation
in an endless bloody fountain
or
learn to cauterize them
into deaf, red scars.

## MÉTIS VERSE, CANADIAN CHAPTER

I never thought a moment of Riel.
Never heard him say:
> You must understand
> there were two nations,
> one large and powerful,
> one smaller and less powerful,
> two unequal nations,
> but no less equal in rights.

Never saw the poster which proclaimed:
> Come to the Golden Northwest
> Home for all People.
> The Canadian Pacific Railway,
> the Grand Transcontinental Highway
> From the Cities of the East
> to Winnipeg and Manitoba's
> boundless wheat fields.

KITS

The Loyal Orange Lodge,
The Imperial Order
of the Daughters of the Empire,
the colonels and lawyers,
accountants and priests
have this kit they give out
marked
yesterday, today and tomorrow.
In it, there are clothes,
attitudes, careers, decorations.
But what if you belong
to a people that has no kit,
that wakes up
at three in the morning
and hears rain
against the glass
and does not believe
in glass?
What if your kit
has been exploded into slivers
that hurt when you move?
What if you wake
at three in the morning
and there is no kit?
There is just glass slivers
in the veins.

WALKING

There are always beggars in town.
My way home is good hunting ground for them,
the streets narrow and thronged with people,
small shops, many doorways.

The men who beg
stand close to the buildings
with caps out,
with palms out,
young men,
old men,
humble men,
lost men.

It is good hunting ground.
Sometimes I give.
Sometimes I do not.
There is no order
to my giving.
It depends if I have some change.
It depends if
I have the energy
to confront
the endless possibility
of my own small soul.
Sometimes, I imagine
it is you standing
on the street corner,
but it seems
the man is always too young,
or too white,
or too dark,
or too healthy,
or too something.

I pass by
or give small change.
And try to avoid
the reflection.

## MÉTIS CHAPTER AND EVANGELINE VERSE

I know my history now, Henry.
I can give it by Métis chapter
and Evangeline verse.
I can tell you about the Acadiens
trying to shake themselves free
of the piss lines of Empires.
Trying to be true to themselves
without wounding others.
Trying to break free from the past
without smashing the future.

It is all there.
I can hold the past in my hands
like a little pile of white,
dry buffalo bones.
But to what purpose?
The diked fields of Grand Pré
will not reappear.
The villages and times of Acadie
will not come back to life.
Evangeline will not have her Gabriel.
The future that did not happen
will not reform.

My children do not miss it.

It is your paintings I take solace in,
not the history.
They feel like home to me.
They have the same sense of a vast land,
and comfort
in being alive,
in being part
of a great kingdom.

Your paintings cradle prairie images
that are warm,
that speak of old days
and old farm lanes.

Paintings that do not forget that
at the end of the day,
we are all refugees
from something.

Paintings that remind me
that the future is now, here
in my own hands,
and imperfect as I am,
I'must make of it
what I can.

Is this where you are Henry?
Or have you chosen
some other road from Batoche?

Have you given up
on the willows
by the river?

NOW

Queen Elizabeth arrives.

She steps off the plane
like a modern Victoria,
the same size,
the same sense
of dense, genteel matriarchy,
the same warm speech:

"My Beloved People".

The past has been re-written.

Gabriel Dumont
rehabilitated from rebel
to bronze statue
on the South Saskatchewan.

Louis Riel
("no murderer,
ever better deserved his fate,")
now hangs as a college poster.

Evangeline and Gabriel
suffer apart no more.
They dance costumed
for summer festivals.
Mythologized from pain
into a dance of continuity
that brings them together
into a dream of yesterday,
into a dream of today.

Yet, it didn't feel like
life had gone on

when I ran barefoot across
the prairie at Batoche,
and felt the soft, deep earth
beneath my feet.
It did not seem like
life had gone on when I walked
along the old dikes,
above the wildflowers and marsh grass
at Memramcook.
It seemed to me as if
I was naked;
as if I was just
at the beginning of my life;
as if the world
was still heaving up
its guts.
Heaving them up,
spewing them skywards
like the heated volcano.
That you and I are the debris
of nations.
That nations are the
debris of the planet.
That our planet is the
debris of stars.
And we burn each other
because we are burning ourselves,
because we can't help it,
because we are children
in the playground
of the Gods.

# PART IV
## IMAGINING ACADIE

What if the deportation of the Acadiens had never taken place? What if the suppression of the Métis had never happened? What if a compromise had been reached between Riel's provisional government at Red River and Macdonald's Ottawa government, leaving the Métis in charge of their own western destiny but accommodating the settlement desires of the east? What if you could rewrite history?

Canada would be a very different place today. Nova Scotia would be called Acadie. The society, culture and economy of that province would stretch back in an unbroken line for 400 years. The settlements around the Bay of Fundy would be older than Boston, older than Quebec City.

Manitoba, the gateway to the West would have had for its first premier a Métis named Louis Riel. The Métis villages at the juncture of the Red and Assinboine rivers would have remained intact because their government would have protected illiterate farmers against land speculators and there would have been no federal legislation designed to break up the Métis communities.

But this is just wishful thinking. You can't erase the brand of history. These things have happened and we are left with the grains of old Acadie in our hands: dry, hard, old seeds which never quite grew the way they should have. And in the West, remote Métis communities are inked with the memory of Gabriel Dumont, Louis Riel, and a sense of injustice that still burns fueling alcoholism and a Métis prison population out of all proportion to their share of the general population.

History cannot change, but it has not unmade the presence of human beings called Acadien and Métis. There are still places which have the heart, conscience, history and spirit of the times before deportation and suppression. I have known this in a confused and inchoate way ever since I used to walk towards the barn with my grandfather as the sun was coming up behind the mountains; when I listened to my grandfather and watched how he did things.

I discovered the Métis when I saw the Indian portraits of Henry Letendre. You could not mistake their soul or their provenance. They came from the place that connects us all under the Great Spirit; that connects us to Wanuskewin and the circle of the sun.

To find Acadie today, you must first imagine it because there is no border to cross, no passport to stamp. All you need is the desire to make the journey and the imagination to pack your bags. You are welcome to join in our tintamarre. This is the noisy, pot-banging parade Acadiens hold every August 15. Its original reason for being has been lost in the confusion of the exile. Some say that it began as an impromptu celebration of finishing the hay harvest, others that it was held as a midsummer folly, to make a joyful noise, to say to the cosmos and our neighbours that we were here and happy. No-one really knows, but nonetheless, there has been a great revival of the tintamarre and everywhere that Acadiens are gathered on August 15, from Louisiana to Caraquet, you will find the tintamarre.

I will wait for you to come, paddling over the water, the canoe balanced like a dry leaf on the clear membrane of the lake.

LE TINTAMARRE

Gabriel Dumont rode by in my tintamarre
and buffaloes galloped belligerently
straight from Buffalo Bill's
Wild West Show.
Clowns
walked with the dinosaurs.
Dinosaurs with long necks,
dinosaurs with sharp teeth,
dinosaurs forgotten from Noah's boat;
and soft-skinned, warm-hearted lions
padding along, carnivorous kings
interested in buffalo.
Behind them walked waddling ducks
and blues musicians,
and politicians promising
and rugby players enthusing,
and hockey players carrying
penalty boxes,
and church angels pushing wheelbarrows
of clouds,
and teachers waxing Socratic,
and farmers with their cows,
and computers with their owners,
and lovers lost in the evanescence
of days so precious
that they were dissolved into the memory of love;
all in my tintamarre,
the earth's parade,
come to bang pots
and sing the song of life,
banging away the pain
of broken hearts and empty souls
and sudden death in the racket
of wooden spoons on frying pans.

The leaves of my tintamarre
are Amazonian,
the colours, a dark green summer day.
Televisions walked with children.
Fishermen walked with cod.
It was an odd kind of tintamarre.
The Holy Grail was there
along with Don Quixote
banging on the holy chalice,
crying in the voice of Yeats,
"Do not love too long"
and so on.
It was a long parade
was my tintamarre
as long as the earth is round,
as high as the earth is high.
And there were majorettes,
whose fathers were majors.
The fathers walked
with rows of war medals pinned to their chests.
They were ponderous,
like fat, old, smelly water dogs.

Their daughters spun sparkling batons
into the air marked tintamarre
and cried, Go! God! Go!
Their legs glistened,
their bodies like waxy postcards.

Evangeline looked for Gabriel.

A white-haired man smoked a pipe
and gazed out at sea.

A woman churned butter.

A foal stood by its mother.

A truck rusted.

A Russian wrote a novel.

An American bought the translation rights.

A Frenchman explained the meaning.

Tall trees disappeared
into Haida poles
where the raven carried the bear,
and the bear, the whale,
and the whale, the eagle
and a man's face peers
out of the eagle's feathered chest
in a sweet evocation
of life's confusion.

Stars above.
Stars below.

All lost.
All found
in the song of the tintamarre,
until the sounds were the sounds
of the salt tide in my veins
without beginning and without end.

But I did not see you, Henry.
I did not see you.

WANUSKEWIN

A deer appears silently
by the water.
Tall, graceful,
she listens for the wolf.
Cicadas buzz contentedly.
The forest aches with warm summer life.

Northern lights
begin to flicker.
Curtains of light
that hang like cosmic fish nets
between earth
and the starry highway
of our Milky Way.

Curtains of light
so beautiful
all the paintings
in the world,
all the poems
in the world,
cannot compare.

They shimmer and twist,
messages of the Gods
misunderstood.

## CIRCLE OF THE SUN

My father taught me,
    rappeles-tu, bien, Clive,
    tu es
    Clive
    à Fernand,
    à William,
    à Arsène,
    à Magloire.

And there I was
tacked on,
an English-speaking,
gangly,
freckled boy,
to the history
of my family,
my place
in the village secure,
for in my grandfather
I would find
the history
of a people.

    Rappeles-tu, bien, Clive.

My children have no
Acadien memory.
They speak French,
but it is the designer version,
created
in the Upper Canada classroom.
Their great-grandfather died
as they were entering
the world.

The farm sold.
The field by the sea
chopped
into lots.
The pasture
under the mountain
gone back to forest.
The old paths abandoned.

They have had a different childhood
with different memories.

They cannot see
the road down the mountain
to the sawmill,
or the new foal
wobbling on his skinny legs,
or the old mare
proud of her last offspring.

No memories of Sunday expeditions
to pick mushrooms on the island
or the long days of
summer harvest
surrounded by the sweet smell
of sun-dried grass
rising in soft clouds
towards the barn rafters.

No memories
of driving the young cattle
up to the mountain pasture;
or stacking wood
against the winter cold;
or clip-clopping down to the harbour

to buy fresh fish;
the fishermen laughing, talking,
home from the sea
for another day.
The air salty with rough words
and scrubbed skies.
The gulls wheeling above the jetty
in raucous, billowing cloud,
screaming, Feed me! Feed me!

My own children have not had the freedom
of another world
and the great, seasonal round.
For them,
the world has been defined
in the fish eye of the television
and the cement umbrella of city skies.

They cannot imagine
walking down a long gravel lane
with one cardboard suitcase
of summer clothes
and their
grandfather's house at the end
of the lane.
A house with no car,
no carpets,
no soft furniture,
no television,
no videos,
no stereo,
just one small radio,
yet to my twelve-year-old eyes
we were rich.

The green fields around our house
were ours.
Each one with their own character
and appointed purpose.
The night pasture
by the barn
for the milk cows,
the summer spring
for the horses,
the hay fields ripening
from sea to mountain,
the gardens by the house,
each field carefully fenced and
tended.

Our house was white and freshly painted.
The kitchen alive with the sound
and smells of the wood stove,
homemade bread, gingerbread and tea.
We were rich.
It did not occur to me that
the house was small and simply furnished
without television or ornament.
I felt the history of Acadie
in the rough, broad hands
of the village,
in the voices of my cousins
and the quick smile
of Gérard à Levis,
in the swing of the seasons
across the land,
in accents and stories
where the order of existence
was defined differently.

One summer,
at Chéticamp beach
a whale got stuck
behind the sandbar,
we pushed and pushed,
pushing him back
to the sea.
He heaved around
slapping his fins
like gunshots
in the shallow water.

What was he saying
with his giant body
and bat voice?

The sea was warm
and salty with August sun,
and we laughed
and laughed,
the sun glinting off
the surface,
surrounding us
in diamonds of light,
and after a while
the whale laughed too
and sailed himself back to the sea.

I love that warm memory
of the whale's life,
and of the future being rich
with possibility.
Rich beyond imagining.
The moment sticks in my heart,

as if the whale had blessed me.
Do you have memories like this, Henry?
That spiral slowly from the past
to the present like leaf smoke
on an autumn day?
That hold the possibilities
of life next to your heart.
That bring the aboriginal
circle of the sun
around to you?

Rhetoric

"My beloved people,
        may God bless you."

It is the sadness
of those words
which haunts me,
their arrowhead death,
for in them lies
a universe of suffering.

"My beloved people"
said
with the best of intentions,
said
with genuine feeling;
yet in them lies
the burning of forests,
in them lies
the massacre of animals;
in them lies
the evisceration of First Nations;
in them lies
the crystallizing of our own
beginning, middle and end.

Can we wait long enough
to redeem
and be redeemed?
Or are we all just parasites
moving from one feeding
to the next?
Burrowing
into the comfortable host of earth,
until the bones of our planet

are scattered and bleaching
on the prairie,
on the shore,
in the forest,
eating our present,
eating our past,
eating our future
until we are no more.

SAINTS

There are no saints
in this world.
Perhaps in
some other world,
but not in this one.
Louis Riel was no saint.
He was not
because he wanted
too much from life
and in the end
that always makes
you crazy.

There were no saints
in Acadie either,
not then
or now.
But there were
many good men
and many good women
and some villains.

I don't think
Father Aucoin
thought he was a saint
when he walked
through the village,
reading from his breviary.
Although he looked saintly enough,
tall and thin
and wearing an old soutane.
When he walked by,
the soutane flapping against his legs,
like the long feathers of a crippled bird,

people knelt and crossed themselves because the grace of God
reposed in priests.

Kneel, cross yourself
and it might rub off.
Like winning the loto.

Father Aucoin
read his breviary, a little,
and watched out of the corner
of his eye, a lot.
Was there a dance
going on at Moise à Polycarpe?
Was young Alex à William
out walking with a certain housemaid?

Who was still working in their fields
in the still embers of the day's end?

Who was watching the sun
go down behind the sea?

Had Johnny à Joe got into the rum?

The village spread out
around Father Aucoin's evening walk,
in paths and laneways, houses and barns
like the lines in his hands,
like bumps in his heart,
that cracked and heaved
and hurt,
and kept him warm
when he was tired
and lonely.

Like Louis Riel
who had the Métis
printed on his soul.
And if the priest was not perfect,
like Louis, it was mostly because
he tried too hard
to climb the ladder
to heaven.

A little sin
would have been
good for them.

It wasn't the priest's sheepdog desire
to herd everyone towards heaven
that people recall;
nor Father Aucoin's thundering
away on the church organ;
nor his Latin and geometry classes;
nor his sermons that people remember;
but that he loved people
and from that single thread
many a thin saint
has been woven.

What are they spinning
from you Henry?
What are they weaving
from me?
From what filament are we weaving
our web?

## Tintamarre Blues

There is a tintamarre
among the stars.
Gods are clanging
around arranging
and re-arranging the universe.
Birthing stars,
extinguishing stars,
spinning stars,
planets and galaxies
on their noses.
Laughing,
dancing,
banging on the cooking pots
of the universe,
whistling down galactic alleys,
radiant, noisy, looking for trouble,
the Gods rumble
and on earth,
in the belly of summer
when our star is still warm
and the hay made,
we have our own tintamarre.
Banging and crashing
down Main Street,
we play like the Gods
echoing sound
back to the stars,
our own noisy joy
that we were born to smile,
to greet life with the open arms
of the tintamarre.
When I am blue,
and have the deep sea cafard,
I think of the tintamarre.

## IMAGINING GOD

Were you ever an altar boy, Henry?
Did you ever chant slowly
through the great dialogue
of the Mass?
I feel it in every church
that I enter,
hear the sound of the organ,
see Father DeCoste
raising his arms
slowly,
his vestments flaring
around him as if he
is a flower suddenly blooming.

"And I will go in to the
Altar of God, to God,
the joy of my youth."

I say these words as thousands
of boys have done before me.
I say them and scarcely remember
what I am saying.

If God is the joy of my youth,
it escapes me. I am busy
looking at the dust motes
rising in shafts of sunlight
from the window.
They look calm, ethereal.
Outside, a country Sunday morning
is unfolding.
In the afternoon, my cousin
and I will play baseball

with our friends
in the cut hayfield.
The day crumbles in front of
my young eyes like cake from
my grandmother's oven.
The boundaries of nations,
of life do not exist yet
and this is a kind of heaven.

The priest replies,
    Why art thou sad, my soul,
    and why dost thou trouble me?

The Mass rolls on
like a great surging tide
from the first words to the last,

past "from unjust and deceitful men
  deliver me;"

past "Glory to God in the highest,
  and on earth peace to men of good will."

past "We adore thee.
  We glorify thee."

past "the maker of heaven and earth,
  and all things visible and invisible."

The Ordinary of the Mass
stands like a great tree
in my youth.
I am grateful for it.
Mystified by it.

Angry with its easy sonority
and many confusions.

I still pray, Henry.
I'm not sure why.
I think it has something to do
with being fearful, afraid of myself
as much as anything else.

People seem to need prayers.

The apostles begged Jesus
to give them a prayer.
And he did,
it is buried in the song of the Mass,
his only prayer,
a few lines,
my daughter calls it
the bread prayer,

> Our father, who art in heaven
> hallowed by thy name;
> Thy kingdom come;
> Thy will be done on earth
> as it is in heaven.
> Give us this day our daily bread;
> and forgive us our trespasses,
> as we forgive those who trespass
> against us.  And lead us not
> into temptation.
> But deliver us from evil.

I say it to myself
in times of great weariness.
I say it because it

clenches the essence
of life.

The bread prayer
asks a little of the world
and a lot from me.

I say it over my soul
the way a Jew
says Kaddish over the dead.
Invoking God without dispute.

I hold my hands palm upwards
to God looking
for a gift.
I hold them palm upwards
like the battered, old man
I met
on a street corner
in Vieux Montréal.
He is missing fingers
and his faced is cracked
and red from the explosions
of alcohol.

I hold my hands upwards
waiting for a gift
that will make sense

of
unfairness,

of
injustice,

of
cowardice,

of
Evangeline's tears,

of
Riel's death,

of
narrow fields,

of
square fields,

of the play yards
of the Gods.

I will accept anything.

I will accept anything,
but money.

This is what
I am waiting
for Henry.

I will wait for it
as the Indians used to
at Wanuskewin,
at the circle of the sun.
I will
wait for the healing
between

earth

and

sun,

spirit

and

water.

I will wait for it.

And, if people choose
to die
in poisonous effusions,
I will understand that
it is just another
rift
in the circle of the sun,
another rift
between us,
another bullet shot,
another Thomas Scott,
another heart broken,
another sundering
of our people.

## THE SONG OF THE TINTAMARRE

Beating the drum.
Beating the spoons.
Dressed
for the absurd.
Ready
to be the wandering Jew.
Ready
to laugh.
Ready
to cry.
Ready
to pray.
In the drum of the tintamarre,
we will beat down the sound
of old greed,
of new greed;
the tintamarre of bile
and terrible thoughts,
of hate
and scrip hunters,
of stealing our land,
of stealing our future,
of deceit and murder
by the crumpled souls of want.
The tintamarre of scars
and asylums
we are beating down.
Beating down
into the place
of deadness,
beating the drum,
beating the spoons,

shouting and hollering
and crying
until the masks
of death are lit,
until the song of life begins,
until another deal
for another year
is done between us
and God.

## WAITING

I will wait by the lake
and
when you arrive Henry,
I will take you for a walk
that will be my gift to you.
I will take you for a walk
along a forest trail
made by my ancestors.
A forest trail
that smells of strawberries and salt.
Where bright sunlight
strikes a mountain stream
and sends shivers
back to the stars.
Along a path that climbs
up into the Cape Breton hills,
where the forest is
supplicant to the sky,
where we are lifted up
past green trees,
lifted up
past wildflowers
and timothy grass,
lifted up into memories
and times to come,
lifted up into the bright soul
of this little planet,
towards a place
where I have dreamed,
the dreams of happy eternity,
along a forest trail
that smells of strawberries and salt.

It is a strange thing
to sit here
waiting for you,
waiting for someone
I have never met,
waiting for our memories
to align themselves
in some perfect order.